WILDLIFE OF NORTH AMERICA

The Coyote

by Joanne Mattern

Consultant:
Dr. Jim Knight
Extension Wildlife Specialist
Montana State University

CAPSTONE
HIGH/LOW BOOKS
an imprint of Capstone Press
Mankato, Minnesota

Capstone High/Low Books are published by Capstone Press
818 North Willow Street • Mankato, Minnesota 56001
http://www.capstone-press.com

Library of Congress Cataloging-in-Publication Data
Mattern, Joanne, 1963-
    The coyote/by Joanne Mattern.
        p. cm.—(Wildlife of North America)
    Includes bibliographical references (p. 45) and index.
    Summary: Details the characteristics, habitats, and life cycle of the coyote.
    ISBN 0-7368-0029-8
    1. Coyotes—Juvenile literature. [1. Coyotes.] I. Title. II. Series.
QL 737.C22M3647 1999
599.77'25—dc21
                                        98-6342
                                          CIP
                                           AC

Editorial Credits
Rebecca Glaser, editor; Timothy Halldin, cover designer and illustrator;
  Sheri Gosewisch, photo researcher

Photo Credits
Dan Polin, 19
David Macias, 43
Daybreak Imagery/Richard Day, 36
Dembinsky Photo Assoc. Inc./Mike Barlow, 10; John Gerlach, 13;
  Jim Battles, 25; Bill Lea, 40
Jack Macfarlane, cover, 39
Lynn M. Stone, 22
Mark Raycroft, 29
Michael Francis/The Wildlife Collection, 34
Robert McCaw, 6, 11
Root Resources/Anthony Mercieca, 14; Franz Camenzind, 26, 30, 31, 33
Visuals Unlimited/Elizabeth DeLaney, 16; Joe McDonald, 20

Table of Contents

Fast Facts about the Coyote

Scientific Name: *Canis latrans*

Size: A coyote is about four feet long (1.2 meters) from the nose to the tip of the tail. A coyote is between 20 and 24 inches (50 and 60 centimeters) tall at the shoulders.

Weight: Adult coyotes weigh between 20 and 50 pounds (nine and 23 kilograms). Males are slightly larger than females.

Physical Features: Coyotes have bushy tails that usually point toward the ground. They have long legs and sharp teeth.

Color: Coyotes' fur may be brown, light gray, dark gray, or red on their sides and backs. Coyotes have cream-colored fur on their chests and undersides. They have black fur on the tips of their tails.

Life Span: Coyotes usually live five to six years.

Behavior: Some coyotes live and hunt together in groups called packs. Some coyotes live alone.

Food: Coyotes eat almost anything. Their food includes small mammals, birds, fish, insects, and fruit. Coyotes also eat garbage and dead animals.

Reproduction: Coyotes mate between December and February. Pups are born between late February and April. Females give birth to an average of six pups in a litter.

Range: Coyotes live almost everywhere in North America. Their range extends from Alaska to Central America.

Habitat: Coyotes live mostly in deserts and on plains. They also live near people.

Chapter 1

The Coyote

Coyotes are part of the wild dog family. A family is a group of animals with similar ancestors. The wild dog family also includes wolves and foxes. All coyotes are mammals. A mammal is a warm-blooded animal with a backbone. Warm-blooded means an animal's body temperature remains the same.

Coyotes are the most adaptive wild dog in North America. They change their behavior when faced with new situations. For example, coyotes change what they eat if the food supply changes. This ability to adapt helps coyotes survive almost everywhere in North America.

Coyotes are the most adaptive wild dog in North America.

Range

Coyotes lived in the Great Plains and western regions of North America during the early 1800s. The Great Plains is a large area of grassland between the Mississippi River and the Rocky Mountains. Today, the coyote's range covers almost all of North America. Coyotes live in rural areas. Some even live near cities.

One reason the coyote population increased is because the wolf population decreased. Wolves kill coyotes when the two animals live in the same area. Coyotes have been able to spread out and expand their range because people have killed many wolves.

Coyotes also have been able to find more food. People cleared trees and created more grasslands. Small animals such as mice and rabbits live in the grasslands. Coyotes hunt and eat these animals. Coyotes also have found food in cities. They sometimes eat pets and farm animals.

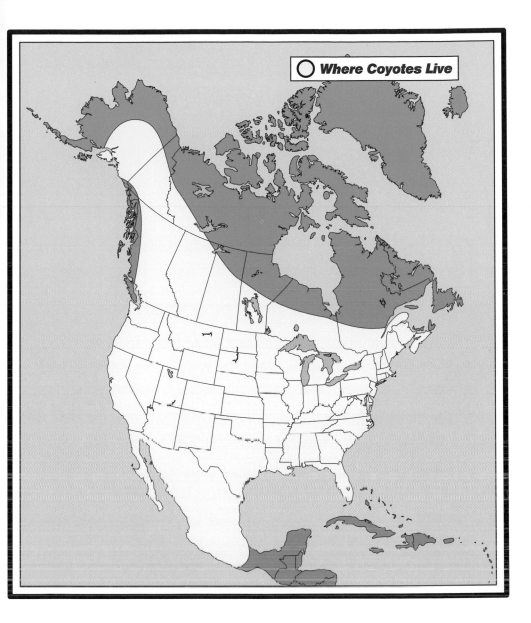

Where Coyotes Live

Coyotes communicate with each other more than any other wild dog.

Physical Features

Coyotes look similar to dogs. They have bushy tails with black fur on the tips. Coyotes usually carry their tails pointed toward the ground. Coyotes are about four feet long (1.2 meters) from the nose to the tip of the tail.

Coyotes stand between 20 and 24 inches (50 and 60 centimeters) tall at the shoulders. Male coyotes are usually larger than female coyotes. Adult coyotes weigh between 20 and 50 pounds (nine and 23 kilograms).

Each coyote may have differently colored fur. Coyotes can have light gray, dark gray, brown, or red fur. Their chests and undersides usually are cream-colored.

Coyotes have two types of fur. Guard hairs make up the top layer. Guard hairs are long and coarse. Water runs off the guard hairs. This helps coyotes stay dry. A layer of underfur lies underneath the guard hairs. Underfur is soft and short. It keeps coyotes warm.

Communication

Coyotes communicate with each other more than any other wild dog. Coyotes bark, yelp, and howl. That was why scientist Thomas Say named them *Canis latrans* in 1823. *Canis latrans* means barking dog.

Coyotes use different sounds to communicate. They woof, growl, huff, bark, and yelp. Coyotes woof to welcome members of their packs. Scientists are not certain what all coyote sounds mean.

Coyotes are known for their howls. They howl to communicate over long distances. Coyotes also may answer the howls of wolves or dogs. In cities, coyotes may howl at the sounds of car horns and sirens.

Coyotes also communicate with their bodies. Coyotes wag their tails to greet members of their families. They bow down and stretch out their front legs to invite other coyotes to play.

Coyotes howl to communicate over long distances.

Large Ears

Sharp Teeth

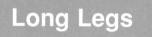
Long Legs

Bushy Tail

Black Tip

Chapter Two

Survival

Coyotes sometimes live in packs. Pack members may live, play, and hunt together. They may share their food. They may share the job of raising pups. Coyotes also live in mated pairs. They may live alone.

Life in the Pack
The leaders of a pack are called the alpha male and alpha female. The alpha pair are the only members of the pack that mate and reproduce young. The bond between the alpha pair is very strong.

The alpha pair has one litter of pups each year. Several pups are born at the same time in

The alpha pair has one litter of pups each year.

a litter. Pups are born in the spring. In the fall, they may leave to form their own packs.

Some pups stay with the alpha pair for another year or two. They become helpers for the next year's pups. They are called beta coyotes. Coyotes also may accept a few other coyotes into their packs.

Life Outside the Pack

Coyotes have adapted to living alone. A coyote might live alone in an area where there are many hunters and trappers. It is hard for a pack to live where there are many dangers.

Some coyotes live alone for a few years. These coyotes are transients. A transient coyote does not belong to a pack. After a few years, transients look for mates and form their own packs. Transients continue to live alone if they cannot find a mate.

A coyote also may live alone if food is scarce. These conditions can lead to coyotes' living in mated pairs. The pairs mate each year. But the pups leave their parents and become transients instead of living in a pack.

A coyote may live alone if food is scarce.

Pack Size

The size of a pack depends on several conditions. One is food. A pack needs a good food source in order to survive. A pack will have fewer coyotes if little food is available.

Pack sizes depend on how many coyotes live nearby. It is hard to find food when there are many coyotes in an area. Areas with large coyote populations have small packs and many transient coyotes.

Coyotes may need to hunt in a large area If food is scarce.

The presence of people also affects pack size. People are a danger to coyotes. Many people kill coyotes because coyotes kill some livestock and pets. Coyotes do not live in large packs where there are a lot of people. Coyotes that live in towns and cities usually are transients or belong to small packs.

Territory

A coyote's territory is its regular hunting area. Coyotes usually hunt in the same area every day. Coyotes may hunt in a small area if there is plenty to eat. This area may be as small as two and one-half square miles (6.5 square kilometers). Coyotes may need to hunt in a much larger area if food is scarce. They may travel more than 10 square miles (more than 26 square kilometers) to find enough food.

Coyotes mark and defend their territories. They may urinate on bushes, rocks, and trees to mark their territory. Other coyotes know a territory has been claimed when they smell the urine. They usually stay away from marked territories. But they may enter to search for food if they are hungry.

Coyotes defend their territories most strongly during mating season and before and after cubs are born. Transient coyotes usually do not go near marked territories between February and July. The beta coyotes defend a territory while the alpha pair takes care of the pups.

Catching Prey

Coyotes are predators. They hunt and eat other animals. Coyotes catch their prey easily

A coyote runs about 25 miles per hour (40 kilometers per hour) when it chases its prey.

because they run fast. Coyotes eat small animals such as rabbits and mice. A coyote runs about 25 miles per hour (40 kilometers per hour) when it chases its prey. A coyote can run up to 40 miles per hour (64 kilometers per hour) for short distances.

Coyotes have sharp senses of hearing and smell. Coyotes can hear many sounds that humans cannot hear. Their large pointed ears help them hear. Coyotes can even hear small animals move through the grass. They often use their sense of smell to find prey.

Coyotes have keen eyesight. They can detect movement well. A coyote may walk past a rabbit that is sitting still. But the coyote will see the rabbit if it moves. The coyote will chase it and try to catch it.

Food

Coyotes are omnivores. An omnivore is an animal that eats both plants and animals. Coyotes hunt for small mammals, birds, fish, and insects. They also eat berries and other fruit.

Coyotes find most of their food by hunting small animals. Coyotes hunt most often at night. They usually hunt alone. But sometimes they work together. For example, one coyote may chase a rabbit toward another coyote that is hiding under a bush. The two coyotes then share their meal.

Coyotes eat whatever is easiest to find. Coyotes are scavengers. Scavengers eat the bodies of large animals left behind by other predators.

Finding Food in the City

Coyotes find food easily in some cities. They steal fruit from boxes behind stores. Coyotes dig up seeds and plants in gardens. They even pick through leftovers in garbage cans. Coyotes also hunt other animals that live in cities, such as rats, squirrels, birds, and snakes.

Coyotes rarely attack people. But they sometimes attack small pets such as cats. Coyotes help people by controlling the numbers of mice, rats, and rabbits in neighborhoods.

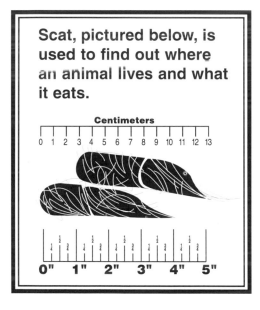

Scat, pictured below, is used to find out where an animal lives and what it eats.

Centimeters

0 1 2 3 4 5 6 7 8 9 10 11 12 13

0" 1" 2" 3" 4" 5"

Enemies

Coyotes have few enemies. In the past, their biggest enemy was the wolf. Wolves kill coyotes. Wolves eat the same food as coyotes in some areas.

But few wolves live in

24

Coyotes find food easily in some cities.

North America today. People have killed
many wolves. Wolves are no longer a threat
to coyotes.

Badgers and eagles hunt coyote pups. These
animals often attack coyote dens when adult
coyotes are not there.

Today, the coyote's biggest enemy is
people. People have killed coyotes for years.
One of the main reasons is because coyotes
kill livestock such as chickens and sheep.

Chapter Three

Life Cycle

Coyotes mate during winter. In a pack, only the alpha pair mate. Coyotes usually mate for life. The same alpha pairs mate each year.

Transient coyotes may look for mates in order to form their own packs. They start looking for mates in December. Several male coyotes try to mate with a female. They follow her. In late January, the female finally chooses a mate.

After the female has chosen, the two mates play together and howl. The pair usually mate by early February. Pups are born about two months later.

Coyote pairs play together after the female has chosen a mate.

Preparing a Den

A female coyote prepares several dens before her pups are born. She does this so that she and her mate can move the pups easily. The pair may move the pups if a den becomes flooded or dirty. They also may move if people or other enemies discover the den.

The female coyote digs dens in areas where dirt is soft or sandy. She often finds abandoned burrows used by badgers or other animals. A burrow is a tunnel or hole made by an animal. The female coyote cleans the burrows. She digs out the old burrows to make them bigger if they are too small.

A finished den has a narrow tunnel from five to 30 feet (1.5 to 9 meters) long. The tunnel leads to a large area about five feet (1.5 meters) across and five feet (1.5 meters) high.

Dens often have more than one entrance. One entrance may be easy to see. Other entrances may be hidden. This makes it easier to defend the den.

The female coyote digs dens in areas where dirt is soft or sandy.

Pups are completely helpless when they are born.

Birth of Pups

A female coyote usually has one litter per year. The pups are born 63 days after mating. Most pups are born in April. The average size of a litter is six pups.

Pups are completely helpless when they are born. Pups weigh only one-half pound (227 grams). They have very fine, light hair. Newborn pups are blind. Their eyes do not open until they are about 10 days old. The

Pups begin to leave the den when they are three weeks old.

female coyote stays in the den with her pups after they are born. She does not leave the den for one week.

After three weeks, the pups have fuzzy, dark brown fur. They can walk by this time. Pups play outside the den. They pretend to fight each other. They chase their tails. They run and jump on anything that moves. Playing helps coyote pups learn how to hunt. They sleep in the den at night.

Feeding the Pups

The male coyote hunts and provides food for the female and pups. He leaves food for the female and pups at the den's entrance. The female and her pups probably would not survive without help from the male.

The female makes short hunting trips from the den after the first week. Other members of the pack may take care of the pups while she is gone. The female returns to the den to nurse the pups. The pups drink their mother's milk for about two months.

The pups' teeth begin to grow at six weeks. They then begin to eat solid food. Adult coyotes bring food to the den. They swallow the prey and regurgitate it at the den. Regurgitate means to bring food from the stomach back into the mouth. This partly digested food is easy for pups to eat. If pups are hungry, they will nip at an adult coyote's lips to ask it to regurgitate.

Adult coyotes soon bring whole animals for pups to eat. They start with small animals such as mice. They then bring larger animals such

The female and her pups probably would not survive without help from the male.

as squirrels, gophers, and rabbits. Coyotes kill the animals before they bring them to the den.

Other members of the pack help the alpha pair feed and take care of the pups. These helpers hunt and bring back food for the pups. They play with the pups and teach them to hunt and to howl. They also guard the pups and chase away enemies.

Pups learn to hunt when they are several months old.

Out of the Den

The family moves from the den when the pups are two or three months old. They may rejoin the rest of the pack. The pups sleep outside. They continue to learn how to hunt by chasing grasshoppers and mice.

The pups begin to hunt with their parents when they are four or five months old. During summer, the pups and their parents hunt, play, and prepare for winter.

Only half of the pups born in the spring survive until fall. Bad weather, hunger, and disease kill many pups. Predators such as badgers and eagles also kill pups.

The Pack

When fall comes, some pups stay with the pack that raised them. They do not mate and raise families of their own. Instead, they become helpers for new pups.

Some of the pups leave the pack in the fall. They become transients. Many coyotes are transients for a year or more. Transient coyotes may travel as much as 300 miles (482 kilometers) from where they were born. Older beta coyotes also may leave in the fall and form new packs.

Transient coyotes try to find mates when they are older. They continue to live alone if they cannot find mates. Coyotes who do find mates settle down in a new territory. They may form new packs.

Chapter Four

Past and Future

Coyotes have been an important part of North American life for hundreds of years. Native Americans told stories about coyotes. In some stories, coyotes gave people gifts such as fire or stars. In other stories, coyotes tricked people. They showed off and tried to cheat other animals and people. And in some stories, other animals tricked coyotes.

A Mexican Coyote Tale

One story from Oaxaca, Mexico, explains why coyotes howl at the moon. In this story, Coyote was about to eat Rabbit by the shore of a lake.

Native Americans told stories about coyotes.

Rabbit pointed at the moon's reflection on the water.

Rabbit told Coyote not to eat him. Rabbit said he had been waiting for Coyote. Rabbit told Coyote he wanted to share the cheese floating on the water. But Rabbit said that Coyote must drink all the water to reach the cheese.

Coyote began drinking the water. He drank so much that water poured out of his ears. But he still could not reach the cheese. Rabbit ran away when Coyote turned to talk to him. Coyote then chased Rabbit. But he was too full of water to run fast. Rabbit ran to a ladder that reached into the sky. He climbed all the way up to the moon. He then hid the ladder.

Coyote could see Rabbit on the moon. But he could not find the ladder to reach him. That is why Coyote sits and stares at the moon. Coyote howls at the moon because he is still angry with Rabbit.

Rabbit tricks Coyote into drinking a lot of water in a story from Oaxaca, Mexico.

Coyotes and People

The biggest threat to coyotes today is people. Some scientists believe that killing coyotes does not reduce the coyote population. This is because coyotes adapt easily. Coyotes have more young if many of them are killed. They mate when they are younger and have larger litters.

But people still try to get rid of coyotes. People hunt, trap, and poison coyotes. In some states, hunters receive a bounty for every predator they kill. A bounty is money offered for killing a harmful animal. People have killed huge numbers of coyotes since European settlers first crossed North America.

Future

People threaten coyotes when they move into coyotes' territories. People become angry when coyotes kill their pets or look for food in the garbage. The best solution is to keep pets and garbage indoors, especially at night.

Some scientists believe that killing coyotes does not reduce the coyote population.

People can sometimes protect their livestock with guard animals. Coyotes are less likely to attack livestock if a dog guards the herd. Donkeys or llamas also can protect livestock from coyote attacks.

The coyote's range has increased. They live almost everywhere in North America. The coyote's ability to adapt to changing situations helps it survive. Coyotes will continue to live everywhere in North America.

The coyote's ability to adapt to changing situations helps it survive.

Words to Know

adaptive (uh-DAPT-iv)—able to change when faced with a new situation

bounty (BOUN-tee)—money offered for killing a harmful animal

burrow (BUR-oh)—a tunnel or hole made or used by an animal

dominant (DOM-uh-nuhnt)—most powerful

omnivore (OM-nuh-vor)—an animal that eats both plants and animals

predator (PRED-uh-tur)—an animal that hunts other animals for food

regurgitate (ree-GUR-juh-tate)—to bring food from the stomach back into the mouth

scavenger (SKAV-uhn-jer)—an animal that looks through waste for food

transient (TRAN-shuhnt)—a coyote that lives alone and does not belong to a pack

To Learn More

Biel, Timothy Levi. *Wild Dogs.* Zoobooks.
San Diego: Wildlife Education, 1996.

Johnston, Tony. *The Tale of Rabbit
and Coyote.* New York: G.P. Putnam's
Sons, 1994.

Lepthien, Emilie U. *Coyotes.* New True Book.
Chicago: Children's Press, 1993.

Resnick, Jane Parker. *Wolves and Coyotes.*
Eye on Nature. Chicago: Kidsbooks, 1995.

Swanson, Diane. *Coyotes in the Crosswalk.*
Stillwater, Minn.: Voyageur Press, 1995.

Winner, Cherie. *Coyotes.* Minneapolis:
Carolrhoda Books, 1995.

Useful Addresses

Canadian Wildlife Federation
2740 Queensview Drive
Ottawa, ON K2B 1A2
Canada

Defenders of Wildlife
1101 Fourteenth Street NW
Suite 1400
Washington, DC 20005

The Fund for Animals
200 West 57th Street
New York, NY 10019

National Wildlife Federation
1400 16th Street NW
Washington, DC 20036-2217

The Predator Defense Institute
P.O. Box 5079
Eugene, OR 97405

Internet Sites

Coyote Facts
http://www.paws.org/wildlife/coyote.htm

Coyotes
http://members.aol.com/ctraisi/fundpage/
  coyote.htm

Desert USA—Coyote
http://www.desertusa.com:80/june96/du_cycot.
  html

Nebraska Wildlife—Coyotes
http://www.ngpc.state.ne.us/wildlife/coyote.
  html

The Predator Defense Institute
http://www.envirolink.org/orgs/pdi/coyotes.htm

Index